THIS BOOK BEL

WHAT'S INSIDE

ANIMALS

Cat

Dog

Mouse

Cow

Pig

Horse

Lion

Giraffe

Elephant

Ostrich

Penguin

Parrot

Spider

Dragonfly

Ladybug

VEHICLES

Car

Bus

Train

Boat

Plane

Rocket

Helicopter

Ship

Truck

FRUITS AND VEGETABLES:

Pumpkin

Pinapple

Broccoli

Apple

Carrot

Grapes

Banana

Cherry

Avocado

Corn

FOOD

Cake

Pizza

Pancake

Ice cream

Cupcake

Sandwich

Popcorn

Cheese

Salami

TREE AND PLANTS

Tree

Christmas tree

Cactus

Bamboo

Tulip

Rose

Daisy

HOW TO USE THIS BOOK

Hello, Young Artists!

Welcome to "**How to Draw Everything**"! This book is your magical canvas, a special place where you can learn to draw all sorts of cute things. Before you start, let's talk about how to make the most out of your drawing adventure.

Find Your Perfect Drawing Spot:

Drawing is fun when you're comfortable! Find a spot where you can sit and draw easily. Just make sure you have enough light to see your beautiful creations.

Gather Your Art Supplies:

To begin, you'll need some basic supplies:
• Pencils, Crayons or Markers: They are great for sketching. These will bring your drawings to life with color.
• Eraser: For fixing little oopsies and smudges.
• Sharpener: Keep your pencils ready for action!

Follow Along and Create:

Each page in this book has easy-to-follow steps to draw different things. Start with simple shapes and watch as they turn into amazing drawings. Don't worry if it's not perfect. Practice makes perfect!

Be Creative and Have Fun:

There's no right or wrong in art. Feel free to add your own special touches to your drawings. Maybe the sun has a smiling face, or the trees have purple leaves. Let your imagination soar!
Remember, drawing is about having fun and expressing yourself. So grab your pencils and let's start this exciting journey together. Happy drawing!

ANIMALS

PRACTICE

Let's trace and color!

PRACTICE

Let's trace and color!

PRACTICE

Let's trace and color!

PRACTICE

Let's trace and color!

PRACTICE

Let's trace and color!

HORSE

Start

① ② ③ ④ ⑤

Horses have the biggest eyes of any land mammal.

PRACTICE

Let's trace and color!

PRACTICE

Let's trace and color!

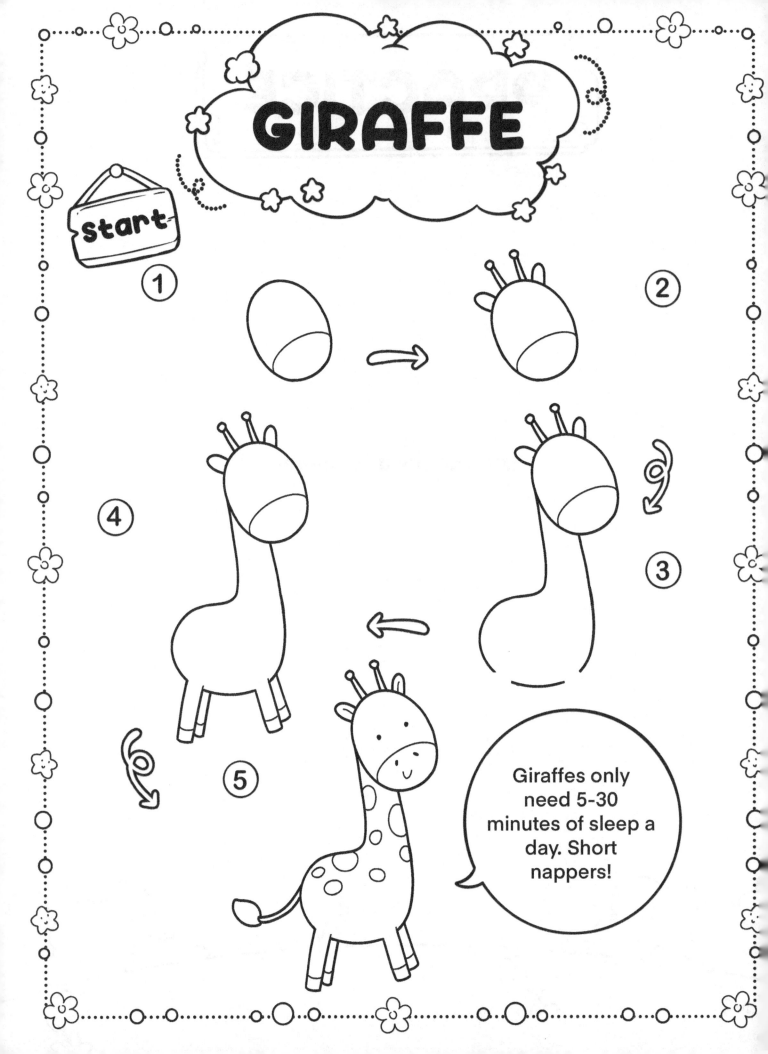

PRACTICE

Let's trace and color!

PRACTICE

Let's trace and color!

PRACTICE

Let's trace and color!

PENGUIN

Penguins can't fly but are amazing swimmers. Birdy underwater acrobats!

PRACTICE

Let's trace and color!

PARROT

Start

① ② ③ ④ ⑤

Parrots can mimic sounds, even sneezes. The ultimate copy-birds!

Let's trace and color!

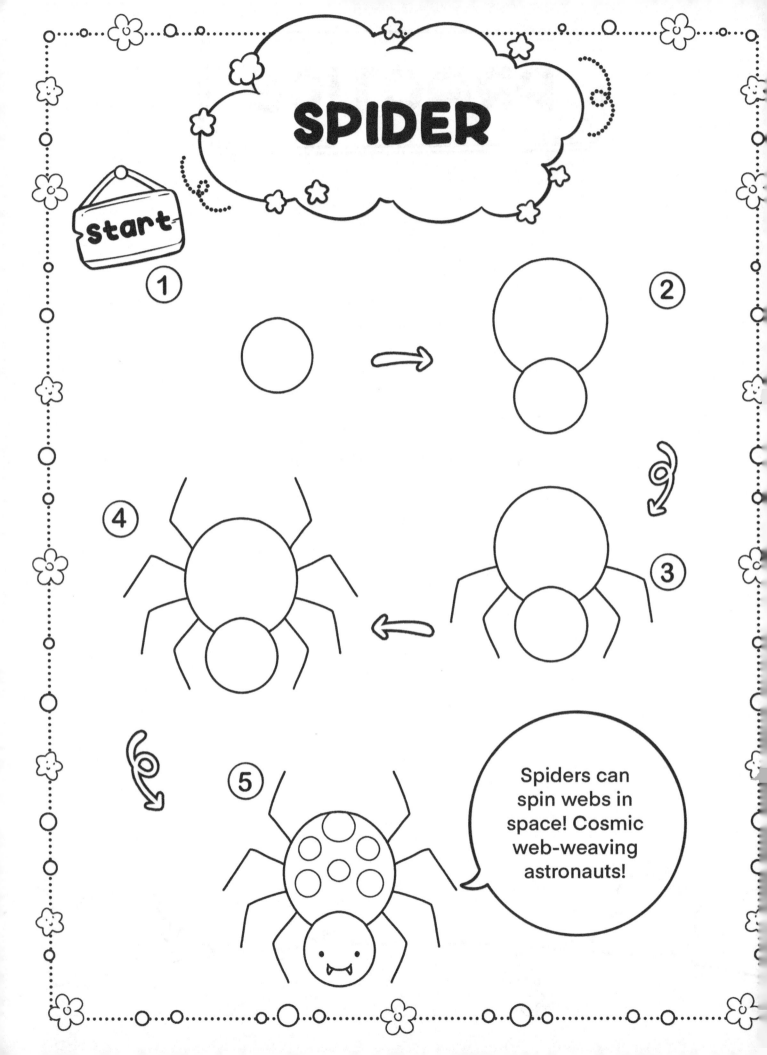

PRACTICE

Let's trace and color!

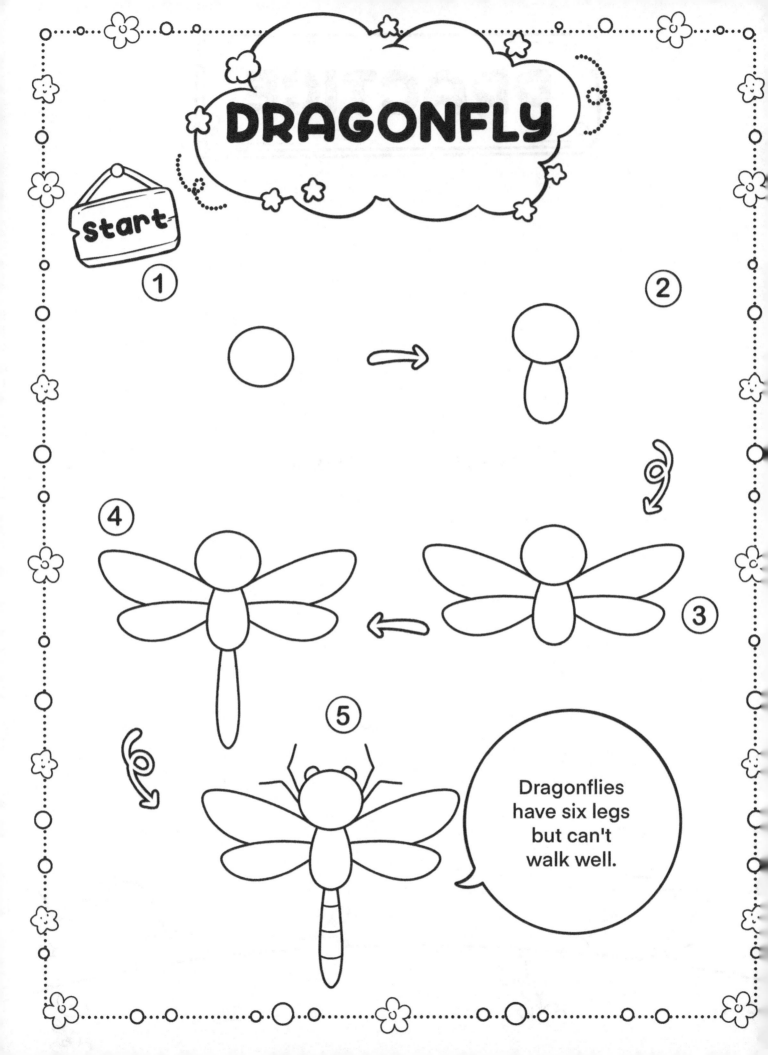

PRACTICE

Let's trace and color!

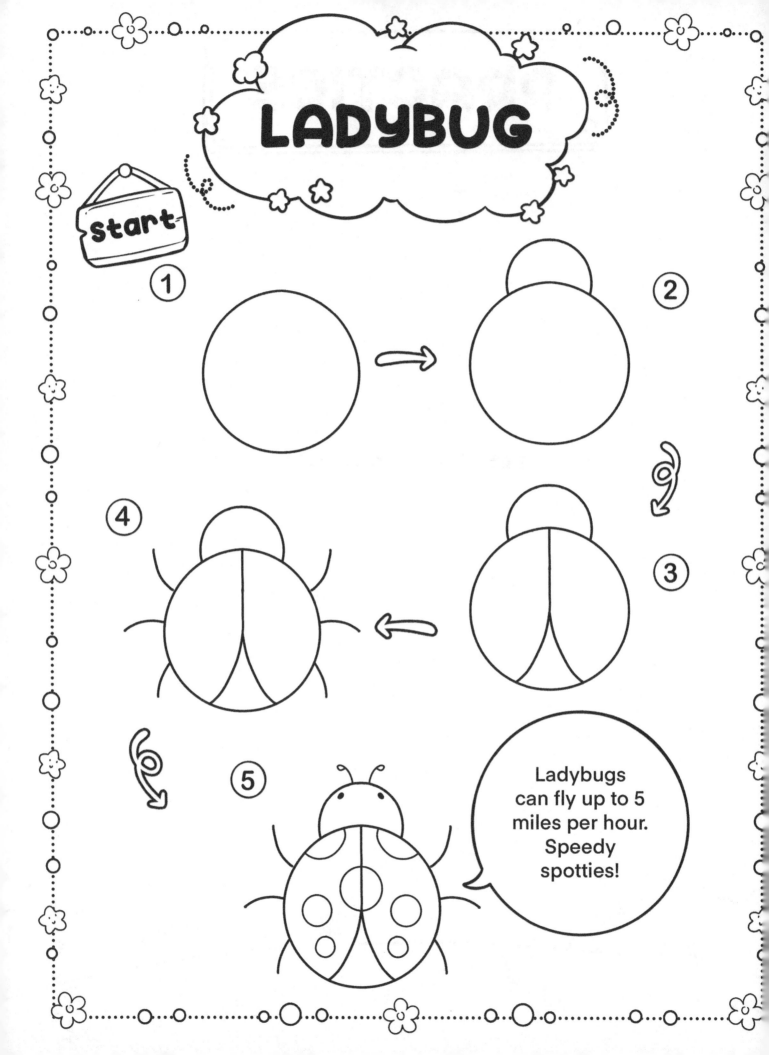

PRACTICE

Let's trace and color!

VEHICLES

PRACTICE

Let's trace and color!

BUS

PRACTICE

Let's trace and color!

TRAIN

Start

① ②

③ ④

⑤

Early trains used steam and looked like giant kettles on wheels!

PRACTICE

Let's trace and color!

BOAT WITH SAIL

Start

① ② ③ ④ ⑤

Sailboats can't sail straight into wind, they zigzag. Dance on waves!

PRACTICE

Let's trace and color!

PRACTICE

Let's trace and color!

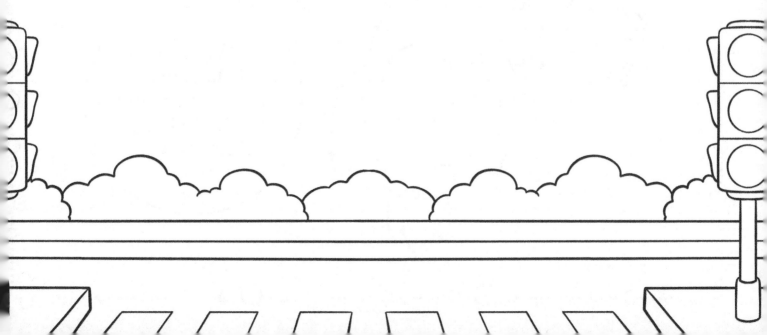

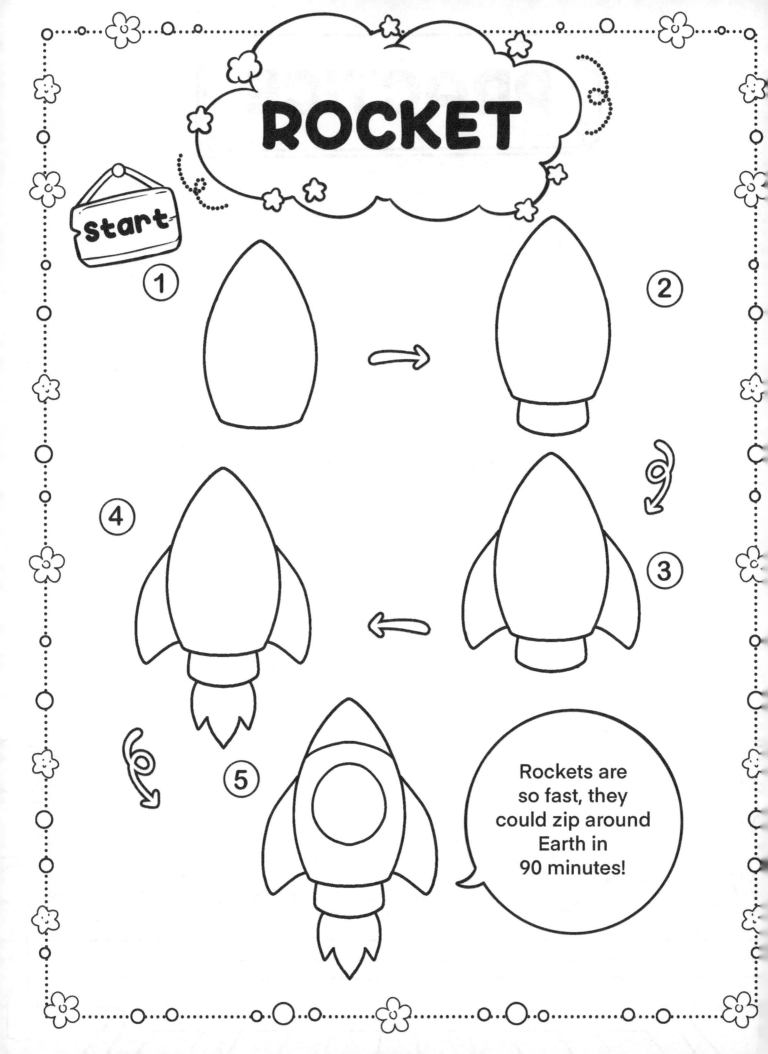

PRACTICE

Let's trace and color!

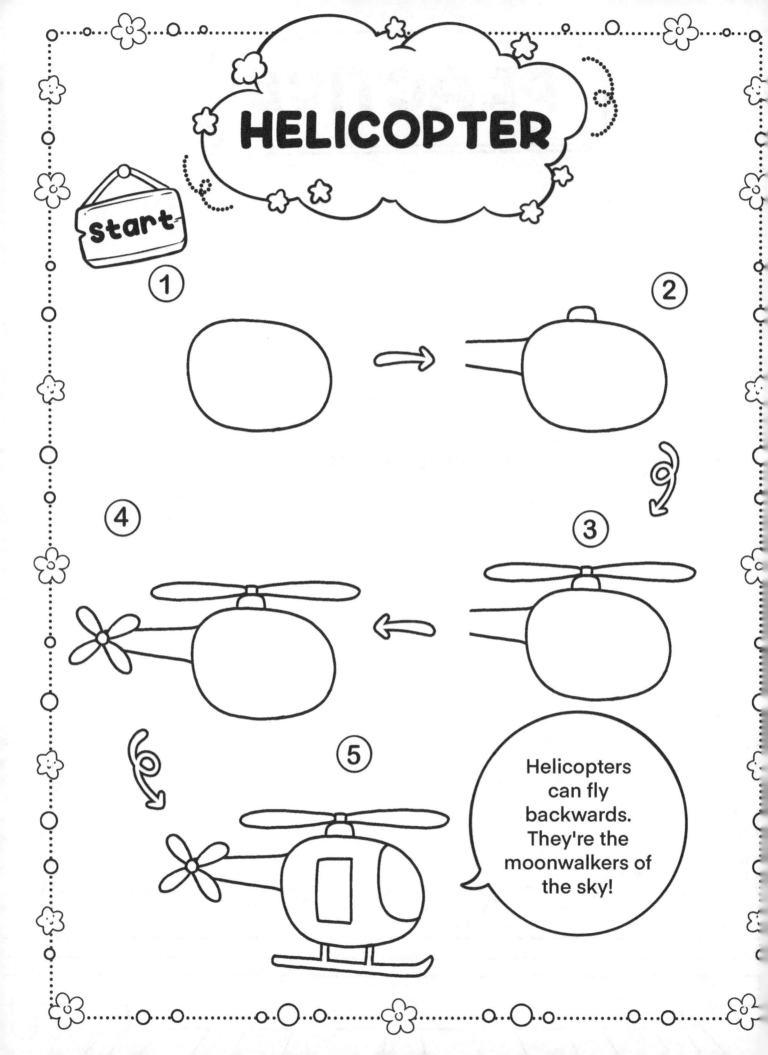

HELICOPTER

start

① ② ③ ④ ⑤

Helicopters can fly backwards. They're the moonwalkers of the sky!

PRACTICE

Let's trace and color!

SHIP

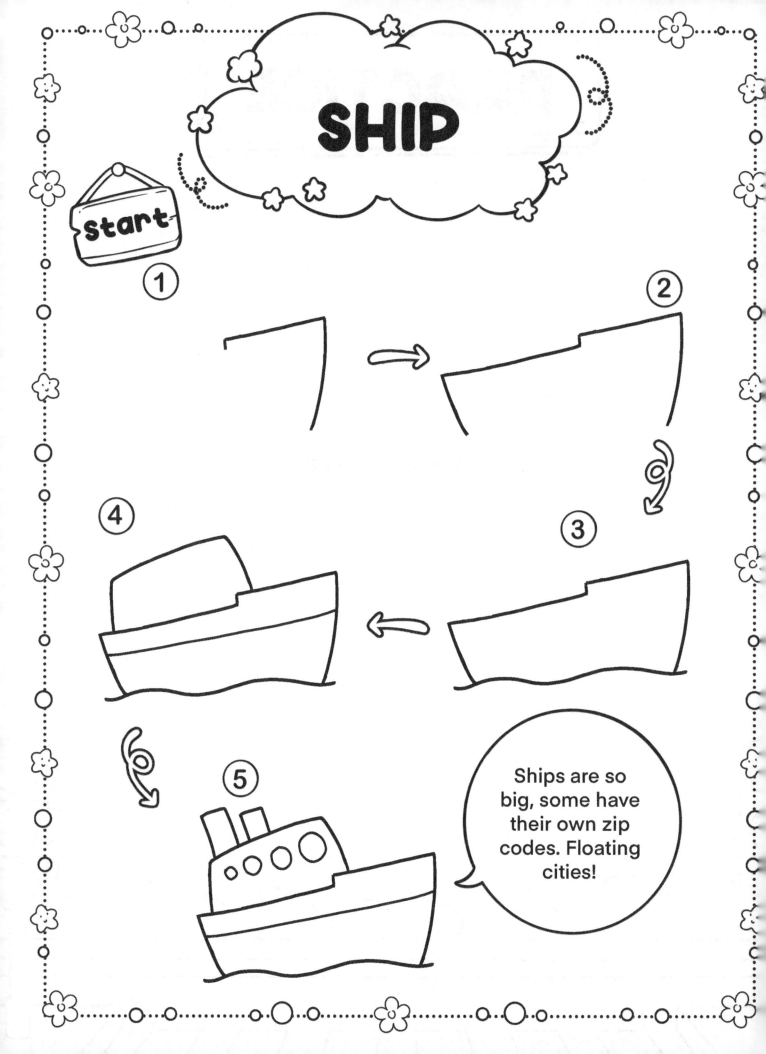

Ships are so big, some have their own zip codes. Floating cities!

PRACTICE

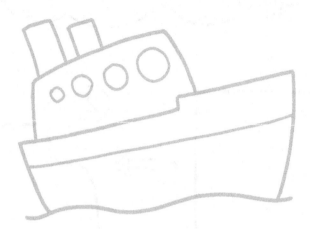

Let's trace and color!

TRUCK

Start

① ②

③ ④

⑤

Trucks can have ten times more wheels than cars. Rolling big!

PRACTICE

Let's trace and color!

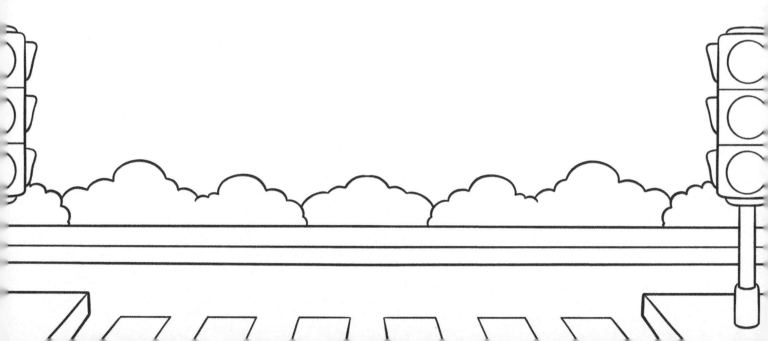

FRUITS & VEGETABLES

PRACTICE

Let's trace and color!

PINEAPPLE

start

① ② ③ ④ ⑤

Pineapples take two years to grow. Talk about slow-poke fruit!

PRACTICE

Let's trace and color!

BROCCOLI

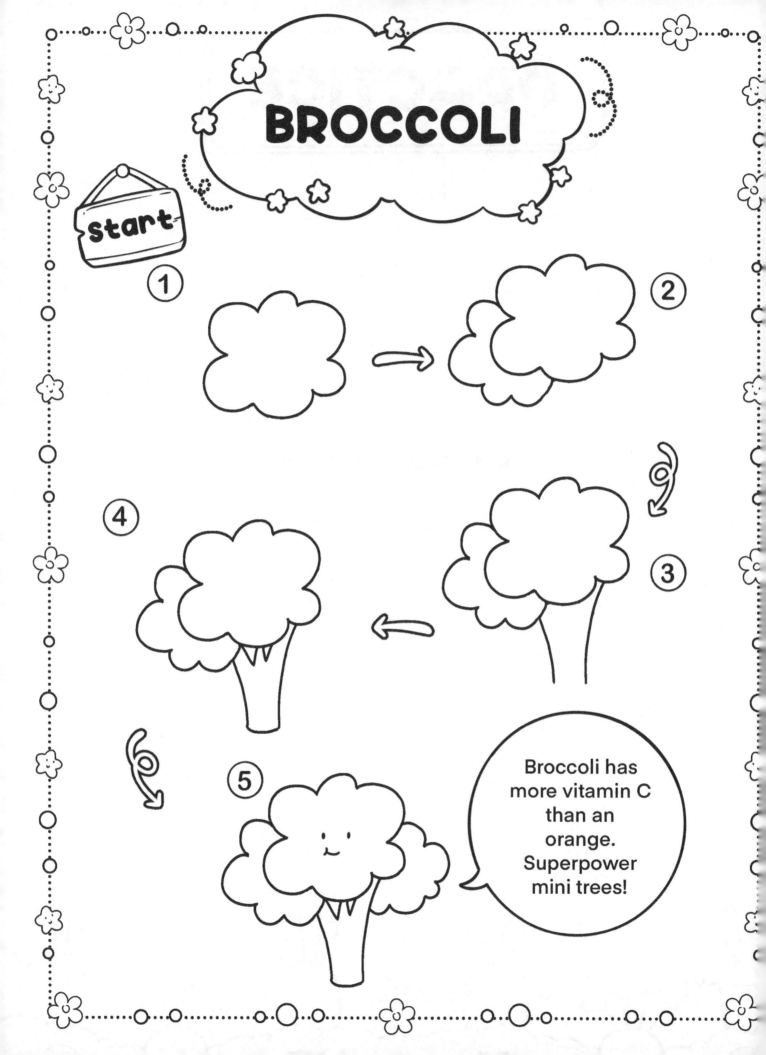

Broccoli has more vitamin C than an orange. Superpower mini trees!

PRACTICE

Let's trace and color!

PRACTICE

Let's trace and color!

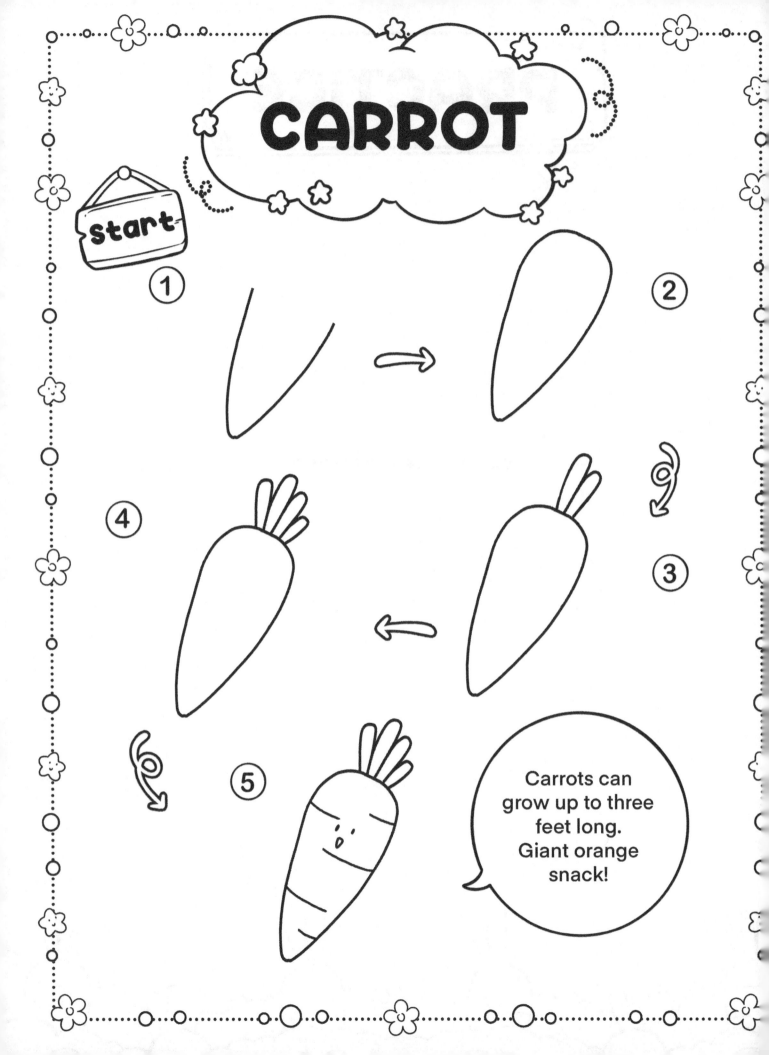

CARROT

Start

① ② ③ ④ ⑤

Carrots can grow up to three feet long. Giant orange snack!

PRACTICE

Let's trace and color!

GRAPES

Start

① ② ③ ④ ⑤

Grapes can be turned into raisins by the sun. Tiny sunbaked treats!

PRACTICE

Let's trace and color!

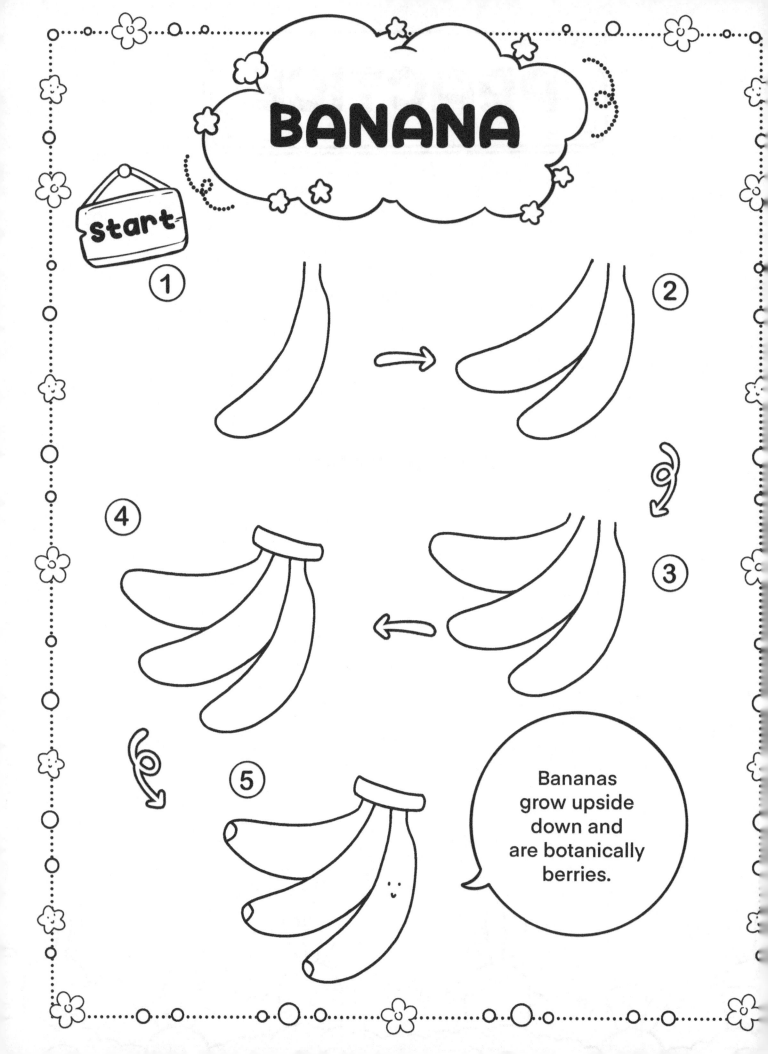

BANANA

Bananas grow upside down and are botanically berries.

PRACTICE

Let's trace and color!

CHERRY

Cherries belong to the rose family. Rosy red little treats!

PRACTICE

Let's trace and color!

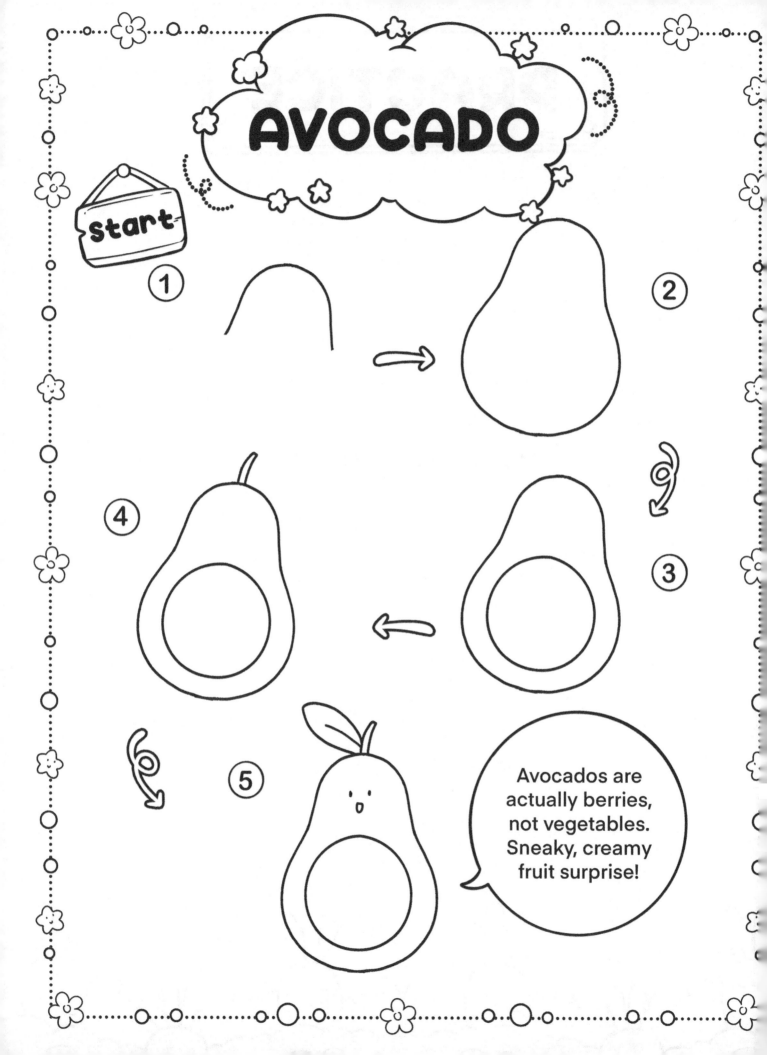

PRACTICE

Let's trace and color!

CORN

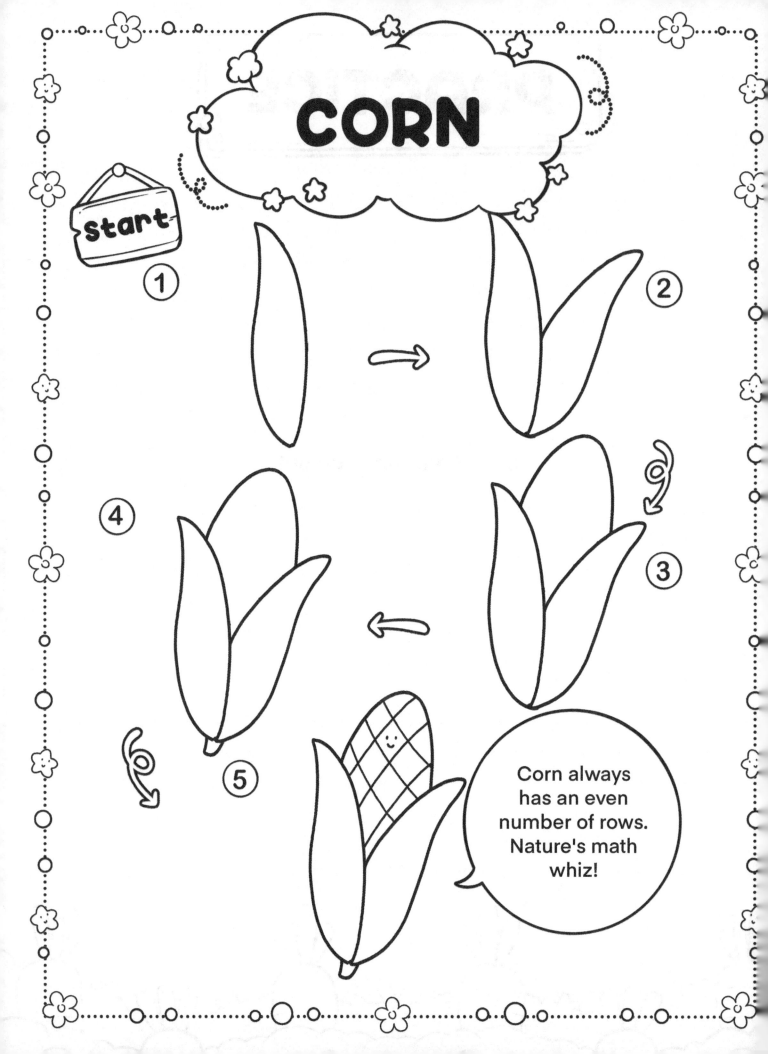

Corn always has an even number of rows. Nature's math whiz!

PRACTICE

Let's trace and color!

FOOD

CAKE

start

① ②

③ ④

⑤

Candles on cake started with ancient Greeks. Birthday wishes, old-school style!

PRACTICE

Let's trace and color!

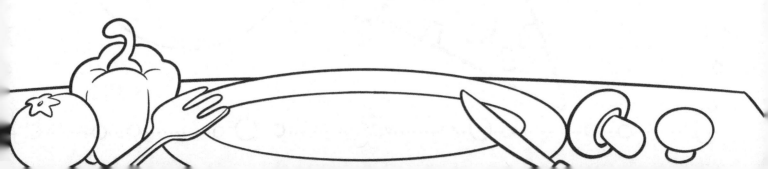

PRACTICE

Let's trace and color!

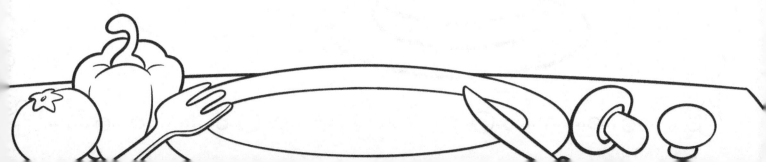

PRACTICE

Let's trace and color!

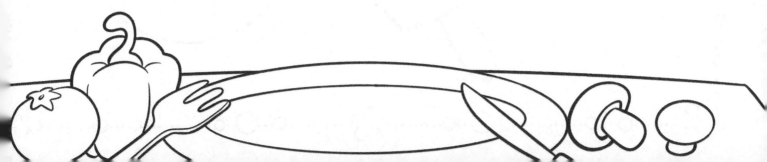

PRACTICE

Let's trace and color!

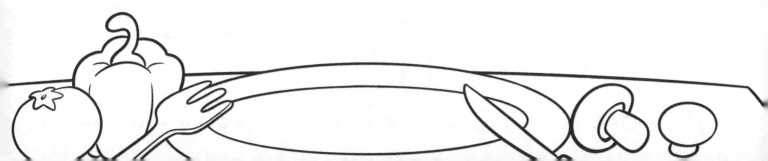

CUPCAKE

Start

① ② ③ ④ ⑤

Cupcakes were once baked in cups. Tiny treats with big flavor!

PRACTICE

Let's trace and color!

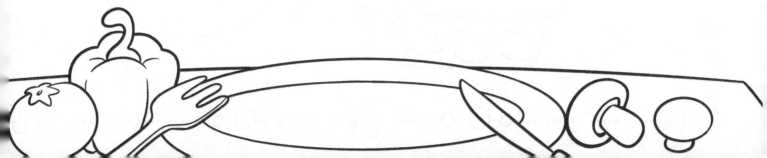

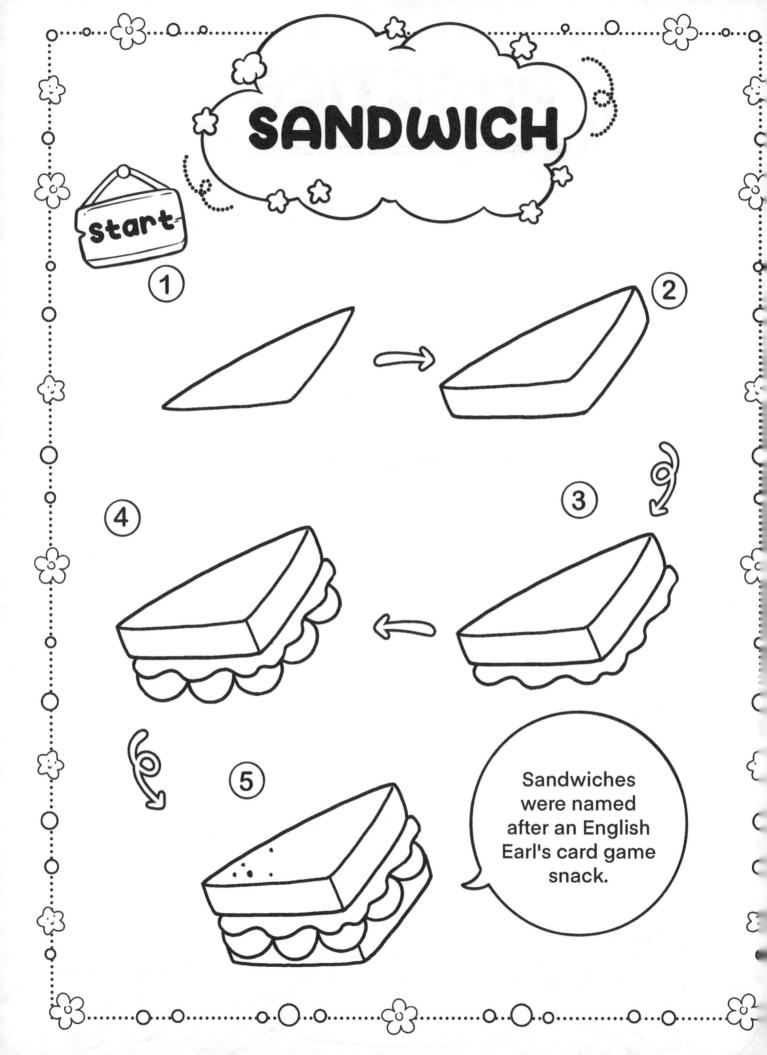

PRACTICE

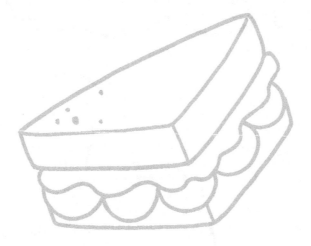

Let's trace and color!

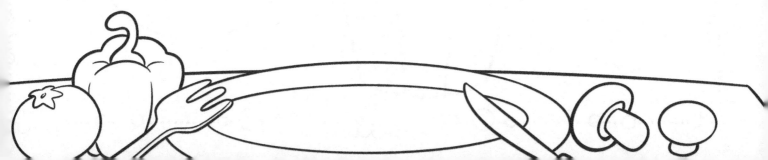

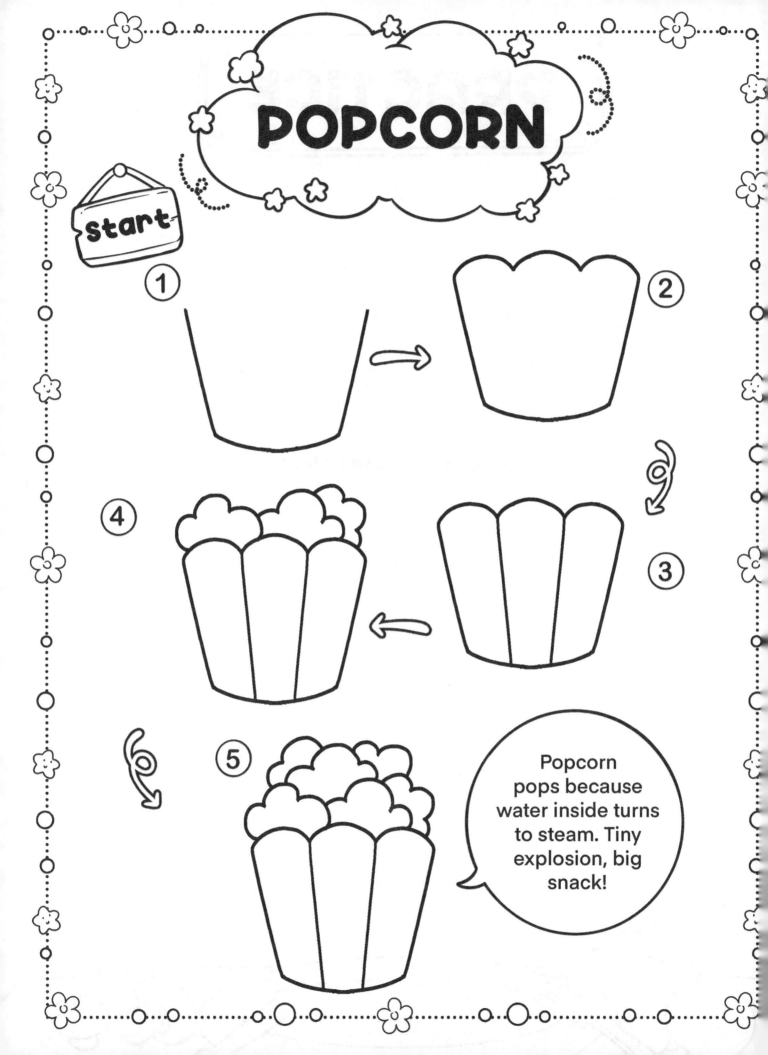

PRACTICE

Let's trace and color!

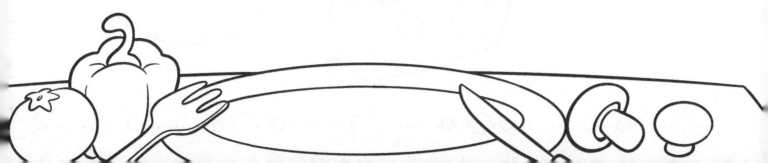

PRACTICE

Let's trace and color!

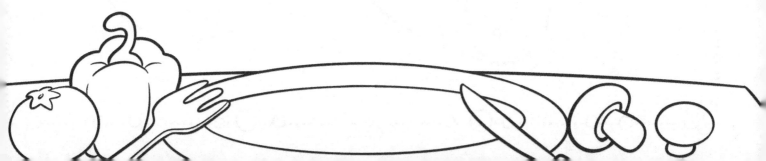

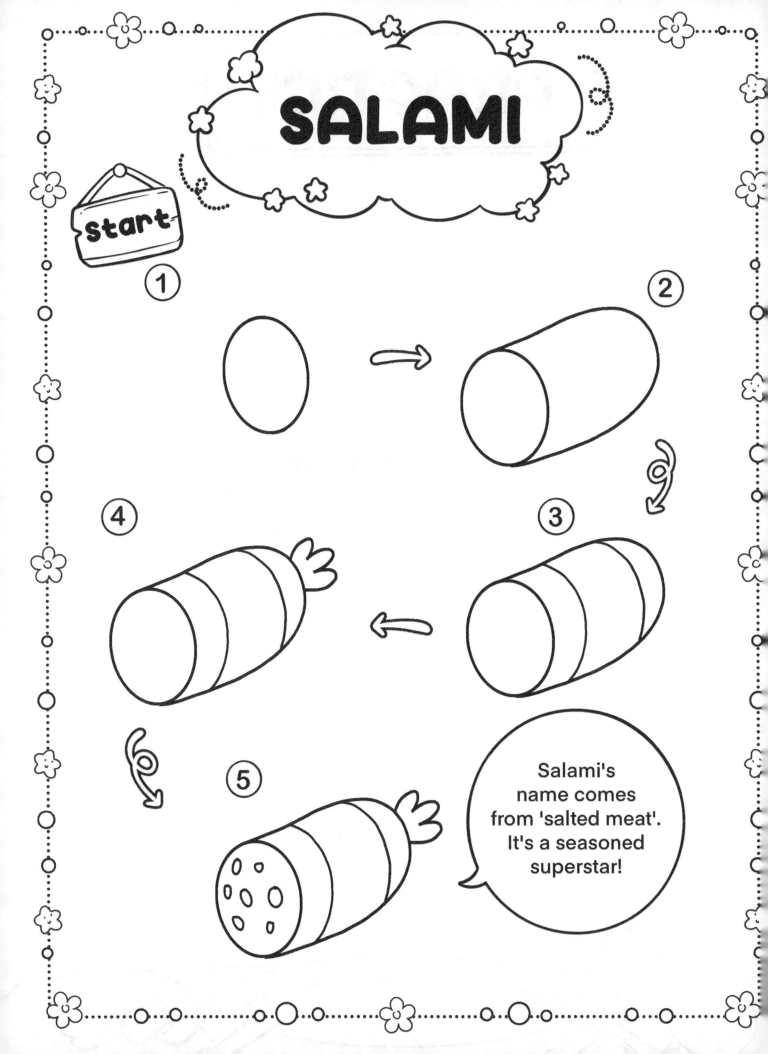

PRACTICE

Let's trace and color!

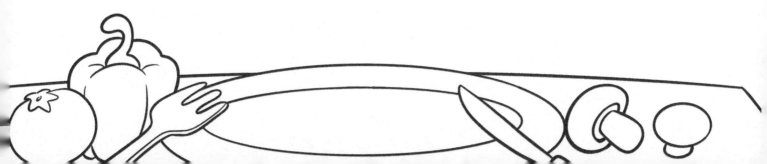

TREES & PLANTS

TREE

Start

① ② ③ ④ ⑤

Trees can 'talk' by sharing nutrients underground. Forest chit-chats!

PRACTICE

Let's trace and color!

CHRISTMAS TREE

start

① ②

③ ④

⑤

Christmas trees were first decorated with fruits and nuts. Tasty traditions!

PRACTICE

Let's trace and color!

PRACTICE

Let's trace and color!

PRACTICE

Let's trace and color!

PRACTICE

Let's trace and color!

PRACTICE

Let's trace and color!

PRACTICE

Let's trace and color!

Made in the USA
Monee, IL
18 December 2024

74284160R00063